A PERSPECTIVES ... K

The Split History of
WORLD WAR II

AXIS PERSPECTIVE

BY SIMON ROSE

CONTENT CONSULTANT:
Timothy Solie
Adjunct Professor
Department of History
Minnesota State University, Mankato

COMPASS POINT BOOKS
a capstone imprint

About the Author:

Simon Rose is the author of many fiction and nonfiction books on a wide variety of topics. He lives in Calgary, Alberta, Canada.

Source Notes:

Allies Perspective

Page 8, line 4: The Churchill Centre and Museum. 9 April 2012. www. winstonchurchill.org/learn/speeches/quotations/famous-quotations-and-stories

Page 8, line 17: Ibid.

Page 10, line 6: World War II Database—Joseph Stalin. 9 April 2012. www.ww2db.com/person_bio.php?person_id=64

Page 11, line 8: World War II Database—Leningrad. 9 April 2012. www.ww2db.com/battle_spec.php?battle_id=125

Page 12, line 12: David Wallechinsky and Irving Wallace, eds. *People's Almanac 2*. New York: Morrow, 1978, p. 95.

Page 13, sidebar, line 5: Franklin D. Roosevelt Presidential Library and Museum. 9 April 2012. www.docs.fdrlibrary.marist.edu/oddecwar.html

Page 16, line 3: William L. Shirer. *Rise and Fall of the Third Reich: A History of Nazi Germany*. New York: Simon & Schuster, 1990, p. 929.

Page 16, line 22: Fred Shapiro, ed. *The Yale Book of Quotations*. New Haven, Conn.: Yale University Press, 2006, p. 154.

Page 19, line 7: History Learning Site. 9 April 2012. www.historylearningsite.co.uk/blitz_and_world_war_two.htm

Page 26, line 11: World War II Database—Chester Nimitz. 9 April 2012. www.ww2db.com/person_bio.php?person_id=10

Page 27, line 11: World War II Database—Paul Tibbets. 9 April 2012. www. ww2db.com/person_bio.php?person_id=422

Page 29, line 5: *Life* magazine, 27 Aug. 1945, p. 21.

Axis Perspective

Page 6, line 23: *The Definitive Visual History of World War II*, New York: DK, 2009. p. 34.

Page 7, line 14: Second World War History—WWII Quotes. 9 April 2012. www.secondworldwarhistory.com/ww2-quotes.asp

Page 7, line 15: Max Domarus, ed. *Hitler: Speeches and Proclamations 1932–1945*, Wauconda, Ill.: Bolchazy-Carducci, 1990, p. 1663.

Page 12, line 9: Second World War History—WWII Quotes. 9 April 2012. www.secondworldwarhistory.com/ww2-quotes.asp

Page 17, line 4: Edwin P. Hoyt. *199 Days: The Battle for Stalingrad*. New York: Forge, 1999. p. 184.

Page 17, line 8: World War II Pictures—Battle of Stalingrad Facts. 9 April 2012. www.ww2-pictures.com/battle-of-stalingrad-facts.htm

Page 17, line 11: Ibid.

Page 19, line 7: Dan van der Vat. *The Pacific Campaign: World War II, the U.S.-Japanese Naval War, 1941-1945*. New York: Simon & Schuster, 1991, p. 139.

Page 21, line 7: History Learning Site—The Bombing of Dresden. 9 April 2012. www.historylearningsite.co.uk/bombing_of_dresden.htm

Page 26, line 4: World War II Pictures—Battle of the Bulge Facts. 9 April 2012. www.ww2-pictures.com/battle-of-the-bulge-facts.htm

Page 28, line 26: Emperor Hirohito, Accepting the Potsdam Declaration, Radio Broadcast, 14 Aug. 1945. 9 April 2012. www.mtholyoke.edu/acad/intrel/hirohito.htm

Table of Contents

THE BEGINNINGS OF WAR

CHAPTER 1

Before dawn September 1, 1939, 1.5 million German soldiers began marching. They walked across the 1,700-mile (2,736-kilometer) border between German territory and Poland, accompanied by tanks, military vehicles, and about 300,000 horses pulling artillery. At the same time German warships attacked Polish navy ships in the Baltic Sea, and German bombs fell from the sky on Poland's cities and airfields.

Poland's people and military tried to resist the massive German invasion, but it was hopeless. Germany was determined to have Poland as part of its empire, and its actions started the largest war in history — World War II.

The German army invaded Poland September 1, 1939.

GERMANY'S ANGER HAS A BEGINNING

Europe was in a shambles after World War I ended. But Germany felt the devastation most. The Germans lost some of their territory under the terms of the 1919 Treaty of Versailles. Germany was forced to accept responsibility for starting the war with its aggressive plans to build up its navy and conquer its neighbors. Germany also had to pay for the damage its policies caused during the war. These reparations had a disastrous effect on the German economy. Germans were angry and turned away from traditional political parties. The situation was ripe for the rise of a new leader with new ideas.

That leader turned out to be Adolf Hitler, head of the National Socialist German Workers' Party, known as the Nazi Party. Hitler used fiery speeches to gain the support of many Germans. After he was appointed chancellor of the country in 1933, Hitler promised to return Germany to its status as a great European power.

Hitler used his speaking ability to rally the German people.

THE RISE OF HITLER AND THE AXIS

Hitler took steps to reverse what he saw as Germany's humiliation. The country began to re-arm and to build a navy, in direct defiance of the Treaty of Versailles. In 1936 Hitler ordered German soldiers to enter the Rhineland, the German territory on the French border that had been ordered demilitarized. Great Britain and France offered no opposition, which encouraged Hitler to be even bolder.

That same year the Spanish Civil War began. Both Hitler and Italian Prime Minister Benito Mussolini sent military aid to the conservative Nationalist forces in Spain, which later won the war. Mussolini also attacked Ethiopia in East Africa, with only slight protests by Britain and France.

In October 1936 Hitler and Mussolini signed a friendship treaty. Mussolini called the treaty a "Rome-Berlin axis around which all

European states that desire peace can revolve." Germany and Italy came to be known as the Axis powers.

Hitler did his best to reassure other countries regarding his plans. He had earlier said that Germany would not invade Poland or annex Austria. But in 1938 Hitler announced the Anschluss, a union between Germany and Austria. This meant that Czechoslovakia was now almost surrounded by German-controlled territory.

Hitler next turned his attention to the German minority living in the Sudetenland, areas on the borders of Czechoslovakia. French and British leaders finally decided to take action and met with Hitler in Munich. But Hitler got what he wanted, and the German-speaking areas of Czechoslovakia were given to Germany. Again Hitler reassured other countries. In a speech about the Sudetenland, he promised, "It is the last territorial claim which I have to make in Europe." In private, however, he said, "Our enemies are little worms; I came to know them in Munich."

JAPAN'S RISE

After World War I Japan had become a major force in the Pacific and the third largest naval power in the world. Japan had ruled Korea since 1910, but also took over the northern Chinese region of Manchuria in 1931, renaming it Manchukuo. Tensions continued with China throughout the 1930s, leading to the outbreak of the Second Sino-Japanese War between the two countries in 1937.

In December 1937 the Japanese Imperial Army captured the capital city of Nanking, China. The battle for Nanking was

Japanese soldiers raised their flag after capturing Shanghai, China, in 1937.

much more difficult than the Japanese army expected, with many casualties. The retreating Chinese destroyed buildings, crops, and anything in the area that the Japanese might be able to use. The angry Japanese soldiers took their revenge on Nanking's residents after the city's capture. Their actions included mass rapes, murder, and torture of thousands of Chinese people.

U.S. leaders were upset with Japan's actions and began restricting exports to Japan. Almost one-third of Japan's imports came from the U.S., especially the scrap metal and iron needed for the war with China. Gaining control of other Asian countries would provide Japan with the resources it needed. Like Hitler in Europe, the Japanese began to plan further expansion of their empire.

AXIS EXPANSION

The invasion of Poland in 1939 was just the beginning of Hitler's plans. Hitler wanted to create an empire called the Third Reich, in which Germany would rule the world for the next 1,000 years. He was determined to provide Lebensraum—living space—for the German people in Eastern Europe. Hitler's blitzkreig, his "lightning war," set the plan in motion. By spring he had added Denmark, Norway, the Netherlands, Belgium, and France to his conquests.

Alarmed, Britain began making plans for war. Britain, France, and the other countries opposing Germany would become known as the Allies.

Luftwaffe bomber planes attacked London.

ATTACKING BRITAIN

The rapid advance of the German army took Britain by surprise. The Germans were able to trap the British army at Dunkirk on the French coast. But almost 340,000 British and other Allied soldiers managed to escape.

Hitler then began making plans for Operation Sea Lion, the invasion of Britain. The Germans needed to gain control of the English Channel between France and Britain and the skies above. Germany's air force, the Luftwaffe, had about 2,500 working airplanes, compared to the Royal Air Force's 700. Luftwaffe commander Hermann Goering was confident, saying that the Luftwaffe was invincible.

The Battle of Britain between the Luftwaffe and the RAF raged through the summer of 1940. By September the Germans had failed to secure the control of the air needed to support a naval attack on Britain. Hitler called off his invasion plans, although the bombing campaign against London and other cities continued until spring 1941. Elsewhere, Italy attacked the British in Egypt in an attempt to capture the Suez Canal. Hitler sent a German army called the Afrika Korps to help out, as Axis forces attempted to conquer the oil fields of the Middle East.

A NEW ORDER IN ASIA

The war in China continued as Japan worked on building what it called the New Order in East Asia. The Greater East Asia Co-Prosperity Sphere was supposed to be a group of nations led by Japan, sharing peace and prosperity. But it was really a way for Japan to control all of the area's resources for its own benefit. With war raging in Europe, Britain, France, and the Netherlands were unable to fight off Japan's actions against their Asian colonies.

At first some people in Asia welcomed the Japanese troops as liberators from colonial rule. But their attitude soon changed. The Japanese regarded other races as inferior and saw nothing wrong with using captured soldiers and civilians as slaves for the benefit of Japan.

Japan joined the Axis powers in 1940. Germany, Italy, and Japan were all strongly nationalist and believed themselves to be superior. All three wanted to create large empires and were opposed to Communism.

1941:
A TRULY WORLD WAR

In 1939 Adolf Hitler and Soviet leader Joseph Stalin had signed a pact not to attack each other's countries. But Hitler had no intention of abiding by it. Early the morning of June 22, 1941, a huge force of German tanks and airplanes invaded the Soviet Union, crossing a 1,900-mile (3,058-km) border extending from the Baltic Sea to the Black Sea. The surprise invasion was called Operation Barbarossa and involved 3 million troops.

Following the German successes elsewhere in Europe, Hitler was confident of victory over the Soviet Union. "You only have to

German troops attacked the Soviet Union in 1941.

kick in the door and the whole rotten structure will come crashing

down," he said. Hitler was determined to crush Communism in the

Soviet Union. He believed Communists had been partly to blame

for Germany's defeat in World War I and that Communism was

linked to Jews, whom he hated.

German forces rapidly advanced across the Soviet Union.

By December they were only 15 miles (24 km) from the capital,

Moscow, and were laying siege to Leningrad. Just when it

seemed as if the Soviet Union would fall to Hitler, the bitterly cold

weather and a massive counterattack drove the Germans back

from Moscow. Operation Barbarossa, one of the largest military

operations in history, was a failure.

JAPAN STRIKES

Hideki Tojo became prime minister of Japan in October 1941 and committed his country to an aggressive course. Even while negotiations continued with the United States to preserve peace, Japan was secretly planning for war. To prevent the Americans from interfering with their assault on Southeast Asia, the Japanese decided to attack.

The morning of December 7, 1941, 366 Japanese planes, launched in two waves from six aircraft carriers, attacked the American naval base at Pearl Harbor, Hawaii. The Japanese also used midget submarines that fired torpedoes at the American ships in the harbor. There was no declaration of war, and the Americans were taken by surprise. The attack sank or damaged eight American battleships

Japanese pilots gathered for a final briefing before the Pearl Harbor attack.

and one training ship and destroyed a large number of American aircraft, mostly on the ground. Thousands of Americans were killed or wounded. Japan lost only 29 planes and 55 men in the attack.

Japan's invasions to the south met with little opposition in the weeks that followed Pearl Harbor. Japan attacked the British-held territories of Hong Kong, Singapore, and Malaya, the Dutch East Indies, and the American-held Philippines. The United States and Britain, along with several other countries, declared war on Japan. Germany and Italy, Japan's allies, responded by declaring war on the United States. The war was now truly global.

By 1942 the Axis powers controlled much of Europe and Asia.

1942–1943: GERMANY STUMBLES

After the failure to take Moscow, Hitler's next target was the oil

fields in the Caucasus region of the Soviet Union near the Caspian

Sea. Capturing the oil fields would cut off most of the Soviet army's

fuel supply, which Hitler hoped would lead to the final German

victory. Hitler was also determined to gain control of the city of

Stalingrad, an important industrial and transportation center

on the Volga River.

The attack went well at first, with the Germans capturing large

areas of territory. The Battle of Stalingrad began August 23, 1942,

German tanks entered Stalingrad in August 1942.

and lasted for months. It turned out to be one of the bloodiest in history. The Soviet troops were determined not to let the city fall, defending every building in fierce street fighting, often involving hand-to-hand combat. One German officer wrote, "The street is no longer measured by meters but by corpses."

Conditions inside the encircled city were terrible. General Friedrich Paulus, the German commander, told Hitler by radio January 24, "Effective command no longer possible ... further defense senseless. Collapse inevitable. Army requests immediate permission to surrender in order to save lives of remaining troops." Yet Hitler still refused to allow surrender. "Capitulation is impossible," he replied. "The Sixth Army will do its historic duty at Stalingrad until the last man, the last bullet."

A week later the German Sixth Army surrendered. More than 90,000 German soldiers were sent to prison camps, where most died of starvation, mistreatment, or disease. Only 5,000 survived the war. Hitler was furious at his army's failure, and the Battle of Stalingrad proved to be the turning point on the Eastern Front.

MORE GERMAN DEFEATS

In November 1942 the British defeated the German army at El Alamein in Egypt, and Allied troops landed in Morocco and Algeria. Axis forces were now being attacked from two directions. The war in North Africa ended with the German and Italian surrender in May 1943.

On the Eastern Front, the Germans managed to recover a little after the disaster at Stalingrad. But in July 1943, they were decisively beaten at the Battle of Kursk. It was the last major strategic attack Germany was able to launch in the East.

During the battle Hitler received news that the Allies had landed in Sicily. Italy's King Victor Emmanuel III removed Benito Mussolini from office at the end of July, although he was later rescued on Hitler's orders and installed as head of a German-protected state in northern Italy. In early September Italy made peace with the Allies, even though the country was still defended by German troops. Hitler ordered troop reinforcements in southern Italy that slowed the Allied advance.

JAPAN EXPANDS ITS EMPIRE

Following their success at Pearl Harbor, the Japanese captured the British possessions of Malaya and Singapore in early 1942, along with the Philippines. Japan also conquered the Dutch East Indies and occupied Burma, threatening British territory in India. The Japanese Empire now covered an enormous area of Asia and the Pacific, with massive supplies of natural resources. Japanese Emperor Hirohito remarked that, "The fruits of victory are tumbling into our mouths too quickly," but the advance continued

KAMIKAZE ATTACKS

Japan first used suicide pilots, known as kamikazes, in October 1944 in the Philippines. Pilots would crash their planes, loaded with explosives, into enemy ships. At the Battle of Okinawa, more than 1,000 kamikaze pilots sank or heavily damaged Allied ships.

A kamikaze attack heavily damaged the USS Bunker Hill in June 1945.

into the Pacific islands. After the naval battle of the Coral Sea in May 1942, both sides claimed victory, but Japan was stopped for the first time.

In June 1942 the Japanese decided to strike a final blow against the U.S. Pacific fleet, as they originally planned at Pearl Harbor. This time the target was Midway Island in the North Pacific, where the Japanese hoped to lure the Americans into a trap. Japan ended up losing four aircraft carriers and hundreds of planes, as well as suffering more than 3,000 casualties. The Battle of Midway was to prove a turning point in the Pacific war. Farther south, Allied forces attacked the Japanese-occupied island of Guadalcanal in the Solomon Islands. Japan was finally defeated there in early 1943 after a long campaign.

Allied soldiers captured Japanese soldiers at Guadalcanal in February 1943.

THE WAR AND CIVILIANS

*J*ust as the British suffered during the Blitz in the early days of the war, German citizens suffered during intense Allied bombing. At least 300,000 people died, with many more wounded. The German city of Dresden was nearly destroyed in February 1945, with more than 25,000 people killed.

German soldier Rudolph Eichner, who was recovering in a Dresden hospital, recalled, "There were no warning sirens. We were completely surprised and rushed back down to the cellars of the hospital. But these quickly became hopelessly overcrowded with people who could no longer find shelter in their own burning

Dresden, one of Germany's largest cities, was nearly destroyed by Allied bombs.

buildings. The crush was unbearable, we were so tight you could not fall over ... Apart from the fire risk, it was becoming increasingly impossible to breathe in the cellar because the air was being pulled out by the increasing strength of the blaze ... We could not stand up, we were on all fours, crawling. The wind was full of sparks and carrying bits of blazing furniture, debris and burning bits of bodies ... There were charred bodies everywhere ... The experience of the bombing was far worse than being on the Russian front, where I was a front-line machine gunner."

Japanese cities also suffered bombing attacks, which intensified as Allied air forces steadily got closer to the Japanese home islands. In the last seven months of the war, U.S. firebombing caused massive amounts of damage to Japanese cities. Although it is hard to know just how many people died, it is estimated that as many as 500,000 people may have been killed and millions left homeless.

THE HOLOCAUST

The most notorious example of mistreatment of civilians was the Holocaust against Jewish people and other groups that occurred in Germany and German-occupied territory during the war. Once in power in 1933, the Nazis set up prisons called concentration camps across the country for those they considered their enemies. They included Germany's Jewish population.

After the war began, German plans extended to eliminating the entire Jewish population of Europe, in what was known as the Final Solution. Camps were set up in Eastern Europe to murder vast numbers of Jews, along with people from other groups, including political prisoners, Jehovah's Witnesses, disabled people, homosexuals, and people who were called gypsies. The most infamous extermination camp was Auschwitz in southern Poland, where more than 1 million people were killed. Approximately 6 million Jews died in Nazi camps during the Holocaust, along with several million others.

The Holocaust survivors were barely alive when the Allies liberated the concentration camps.

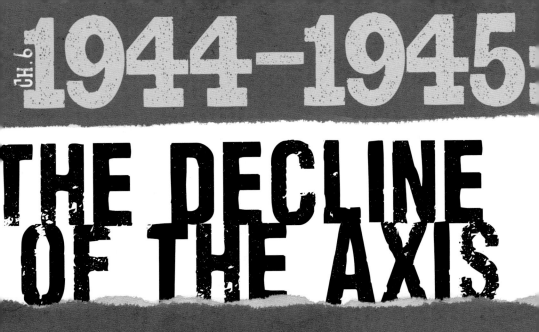

THE DECLINE
OF THE AXIS

The war was not going well for Germany in 1944. The Soviet army was moving in from the east, and the Allies continued to advance in Italy, capturing Rome in early June. The Allied invasion of northern France, called D-Day, began June 6. Faulty intelligence led German leaders to believe the biggest Allied assault would be at Pas-de-Calais, France. They stationed the majority of their forces there. Instead, the invasion came at the beaches of Normandy, about 150 miles (241 km) southwest. By the time the Germans realized their mistake, it was too late to stop the Allies.

Captured German soldiers marched through the streets of Aachen, Germany, in October 1944.

In August Germany was also forced to retreat when the Allies launched an invasion of southern France. Germany was now fighting a war on three fronts—in the East, in Italy, and in France. The German armies retreated during battles that raged throughout the summer. By fall they had been pushed back to the borders of Belgium, the Netherlands, and Germany itself. And Soviet forces had entered Romania, Bulgaria, Hungary, and Poland.

Despite these setbacks, Hitler was determined to stop the Allied forces in the West. In late 1944 the Germans began a major attack against the Allies in Belgium and Luxembourg. Hitler's goal was to split the Allied forces and capture the Belgian port of Antwerp, which served Allied supply ships. The attack became known as the Battle of the Bulge because the German attack created a bulge in the Allied front line. The attack was risky—Germany was running low on military supplies. "We gamble everything now," General Gerd von Rundstedt advised Hitler. "We cannot fail."

On December 16 German soldiers began their attack in a thick fog. The weather prevented Allied planes from flying, and the German forces pushed U.S. troops back almost to the Meuse River. German soldiers also surrounded the American-held town of Bastogne. But once the weather cleared, it was a different story. The Germans faced the full force of Allied air power. Estimated German casualties in the Battle of the Bulge were 60,000 to 100,000.

GERMANY NEARS THE END

German commanders knew that the war was lost, but Hitler refused to give up. He was determined to fight to the last. The situation continued to worsen for Germany. German forces were pushed back to the Rhine River. The Allies then crossed the river and entered western Germany. They continued to move into the heart of the country. The Soviet army advanced into eastern Germany and surrounded Berlin by the end of April. By this time many German civilians were fleeing west to avoid being captured by the Soviets.

As Soviet troops fought what was left of the German army in Berlin, Hitler huddled in a bunker underneath his headquarters, along with his staff and closest military advisers. Hitler and his wife committed suicide April 30. Other Nazi leaders also committed suicide. Director of propaganda, Joseph Goebbels, and his wife poisoned their six young children before killing themselves. Berlin surrendered May 2, and the official surrender of all German forces took place May 8, ending World War II in Europe.

Ruins surround a German officer in Saarbrücken, Germany.

The Germans had come to realize that their cause was hopeless, but they were still in a state of shock at their defeat. Hitler and the Nazis had enjoyed a great deal of support and had been part of people's lives since 1933. The Third Reich had come crashing down, leaving a huge void. And yet all around them, the Germans could see what the Nazis had brought them. Germany was in ruins, millions were dead, and the country was under foreign occupation. Germans were relieved that the war was over but realized that it would take years for their country to rebuild and recover.

SETBACKS IN THE PACIFIC

In Asia Japan faced a major Allied offensive in the central Pacific, resulting in the loss of the Gilbert and Marshall islands and Guam. In mid-June 1944 U.S. forces landed on Saipan in the Mariana

Islands. After fierce fighting almost all 30,000 Japanese defenders were dead, along with about 20,000 civilians. In October U.S. forces invaded the Philippines.

Japan's leaders were badly shaken by the loss of Saipan. The shame of the defeat caused Tojo to resign as prime minister. In February 1945 the Americans launched their first attack on Japanese soil at the island of Iwo Jima. The battle was one of the bloodiest of the Pacific war, with heavy Japanese casualties. Japanese soldiers often committed suicide rather than be captured, believing there was no honor in surrender. In April the Allies invaded the island of Okinawa, located 340 miles (547 km) south of Japan. Okinawa fell to the Allies in June. About 110,000 Japanese soldiers and 45,000 civilians were killed.

Japan's cities were suffering from heavy American bombing, while U.S. submarines steadily cut off all of Japan's imports. But although the war seemed lost, the Japanese government was determined to resist. An Allied invasion of Japan was expected in the fall, but in August a series of events finally persuaded Japan to surrender.

On August 6, 1945, the United States attacked the city of Hiroshima with an atomic bomb, killing about 70,000 people. On August 8 the Soviet Union attacked the Japanese army based in Manchuria, China. The next day the Americans dropped an atomic bomb on the city of Nagasaki, killing about 50,000. The Japanese government then decided to surrender, with Emperor Hirohito broadcasting the decision to the nation August 15. "Should we

The attacks on Hiroshima (above) and Nagasaki devastated Japan.

continue to fight," he said, "it would not only result in an ultimate collapse and obliteration of the Japanese nation, but also it would lead to the total extinction of human civilization."

A large crowd of weeping Japanese gathered in front of the imperial palace in Tokyo. Many military officers and civilians committed suicide. Japanese soldiers, who were enraged by the surrender, also killed some Allied prisoners. Japanese cities had been bombed beyond recognition, food was scarce, and the country's transportation system and economy were in ruins. The Japanese people faced years of hardship before their country could begin to recover. The official surrender documents were signed September 2, 1945, on the USS *Missouri* in Tokyo Bay, ending the war at last.

INDEX

Select Bibliography

Barraclough, Geoffrey, ed. *The Times Atlas of World History*. London: Times Books, 1989.

Cross, Robin. *Fallen Eagle: The Last Days of the Third Reich*. New York: John Wiley & Sons, 1995.

History Learning Site: World War II. 20 April 2012. www.historylearningsite.co.uk/world%20war%20two.htm

Opie, Robert. *The Wartime Scrapbook: From Blitz to Victory, 1939–1945*. London: New Cavendish, 1995.

Overy, R.J. *The Penguin Historical Atlas of the Third Reich*. London: Penguin Books Ltd., 1996.

Overy, R.J. *Why the Allies Won*. New York: W.W. Norton, 1995.

Second World War History. 20 April 2012. www.secondworldwarhistory.com/ww2-quotes.asp

Sturgeon, Alison, ed. *World War II: The Definitive Visual History: From Blitzkrieg to the Atom Bomb*. New York: DK Pub., 2009.

Further Reading

Bliven, Bruce Jr. *Invasion: The Story of D-Day*. New York: Sterling Publishing, 2007.

Grant, R.G. *World War II: The Events and Their Impact on Real People*. New York: DK Pub., 2008.

Fitzgerald, Stephanie. *Pearl Harbor: Day of Infamy*. Minneapolis: Compass Point Books, 2006.

McNeese, Tim. *World War II, 1939–1945*. New York: Chelsea House, 2010.

September 8: Siege of Leningrad begins; it will last 872 days

December 7: Japan attacks the U.S. naval base at Pearl Harbor, Hawaii

December 8: U.S. declares war on Japan

1942

January–April: Japan invades the Philippines, Singapore, Dutch East Indies, and Burma

May 4–8: Japan retreats after the Battle of the Coral Sea

June 4–7: U.S. defeats Japan at the Battle of Midway

August 23: Battle of Stalingrad begins

October 23–November 11: Allies defeat Germany at the Battle of El Alamein

1945

February 19–March 26: U.S. defeats Japan at the Battle of Iwo Jima

April 1–June 21: Allies defeat Japan at the Battle of Okinawa

April 28: Mussolini is executed in Italy

April 30: Hitler commits suicide in Berlin

May 8: Germany surrenders

August 6: U.S. drops an atomic bomb on Hiroshima, Japan

August 8: Soviets enter the war against Japan

August 9: U.S. drops an atomic bomb on Nagasaki, Japan

September 2: Japan formally surrenders

TIMELINE

1939

September 1: Germany invades Poland

September 3: Britain and France declare war on Germany

1940

April: Germany invades Denmark and Norway

May: German blitzkrieg overwhelms Belgium, the Netherlands, and France

June 22: France surrenders to Germany

July to September: Battle of Britain

September: London Blitz begins; Italy invades Egypt

1941

June 22: Germany invades the Soviet Union, known as Operation Barbarossa

1943

February 2: Battle of Stalingrad ends with a Soviet victory over Germany

May: Axis surrender in North Africa

July: Allies invade Sicily; Mussolini is removed from power

July 5–August 23: Soviets defeat Germany at the Battle of Kursk

September: Allies invade Italy; the Italians surrender; German troops move into Italy

1944

June 4: Rome falls to the Allies

June 6: Allies invade northern France on D–Day

June 15–July 9: Allies defeat Japan in the Battle of Saipan

December 16: Battle of the Bulge begins

GLOSSARY

ALLIANCE—an agreement between nations to work together

CASUALTIES—people killed, wounded, or missing in a battle or war

COMMUNISM—system in which goods and property are owned by the government and shared in common; Communist rulers limit personal freedoms to achieve their goals

EASTERN FRONT—the course of World War II in Eastern Europe and Russia

INFAMY—a lasting, widespread, and deep-rooted evil reputation brought about by something criminal, shocking, or brutal

KAMIKAZE—a Japanese suicide pilot

NATIONALIST—a person who believes in promoting his or her country's culture and interests over all other countries

OFFENSIVE—an organized military attack

REPARATION—payments made to make amends for wrongdoing

SIEGE—an attack designed to surround a place and cut it off from supplies or help, in order to force surrender

TREATY—a formal agreement between groups or nations

-I-

INTERNET SITES

Use FactHound to find Internet sites related to this book. All of the sites on FactHound have been researched by our staff.

Here's all you do:

Visit *www.facthound.com*

Type in this code: 9780756545697

A Perspectives Flip Book

The Split History of

World War II

Allies Perspective

By Simon Rose

Content Consultant:
Timothy Solie
Adjunct Professor
Department of History
Minnesota State University, Mankato

COMPASS POINT BOOKS
a capstone imprint

Compass Point Books
1710 Roe Crest Drive
North Mankato, Minnesota 56003
www.capstonepub.com

Library of Congress Cataloging-in-Publication Data
Rose, Simon, 1961–
The split history of World War II : a perspectives flip book / by Simon Rose.
p. cm. — (Perspectives flip book)
Includes bibliographical references and index.
Summary: "Describes the opposing viewpoints of the Allies and Axis during World War II"
—Provided by publisher.
ISBN 978-0-7565-4569-7 (library binding)
ISBN 978-0-7565-4598-7 (paperback)
ISBN 978-0-7565-4632-8 (ebook PDF)
1. World War, 1939-1945 —Juvenile literature. I. Title.
D743.7.R67 2013
940.53 —dc23   20120047452012004681

EDITOR
ANGIE KAELBERER

DESIGNER
ASHLEE SUKER

MEDIA RESEARCHER
WANDA WINCH

LIBRARY CONSULTANT
KATHLEEN BAXTER

PRODUCTION SPECIALIST
MICHELLE BIEDSCHEID

IMAGE CREDITS
Allies Perspective: Alamy: Lordprice Collection, 17; AP Images, 11; Corbis: Bettmann, cover
(bottom), 13, 15; Library of Congress: Prints and Photographs Division, 23, 28; National
Archives and Records Administration (NARA), 9, 20, 25, U.S. Navy photo by Joe Rosenthal, 26,
U.S. Navy photo by Lt. Victor Jorgensen, 29; Naval Historical Foundation, 5, 18; SuperStock
Inc: Everett Collection, cover (top)

Axis Perspective: Corbis: Bettmann, cover (top), 20, dpa/Archiv/Berliner Verlag, 17, Hulton-
Deutsch Collection, 10, 22; Getty Images Inc: Keystone, 14, 19, Pictorial Parade, 5; Library of
Congress: Prints and Photographs Division, 6; National Archives and Records Administration
(NARA),13, 25, 27, U.S. Army photo by Lt. A.E. Samuelson, 23; Newscom: akg-images, 8,
Album, 29; SuperStock Inc: Everett Collection, cover (bottom)

Art elements: Shutterstock: Color Symphony, paper texture, Ebtikar, flag, Sandra Cunningham,
grunge photo, SvetlanaR, grunge lines

Printed in the United States of America in Stevens Point, Wisconsin.
042012   006678WZF12

Table of Contents

SHARED RESOURCES

PRELUDE TO WAR

December 7, 1941, dawned as a typical Sunday at the U.S. Navy base in Pearl Harbor, Hawaii. Many sailors were on shore leave, some were still in bed or eating breakfast, and a few were on duty aboard the warships docked in the harbor.

At 7:55 a.m. that peaceful day was shattered. Japanese planes roared through the sky over the harbor, raining deadly bombs in a surprise attack. Two hours later more than 2,400 Americans were dead, and the United States was plunged into the most devastating war the world has ever seen — World War II.

Japanese bombs sank the USS West Virginia *at Pearl Harbor.*

BEGINNINGS OF WAR

World War II actually began in September 1939, but the United States managed to stay out of it until the attack on Pearl Harbor. U.S. allies such as France and Great Britain, however, were part of the war from the beginning.

The seeds of the war were sown more than 20 years earlier, at the end of World War I. When the Treaty of Versailles was signed in 1919, many people breathed a sigh of relief. After years of fighting and more than 15 million deaths, the world was at peace.

But not everyone was pleased—especially the Germans, who lost the war. The treaty forced Germany to give up much of its territory and all of its colonies. Germany was also forced to pay for the cost of the conflict. Resentment at the treaty terms would be a key

part of the rise of Adolf Hitler and the National Socialist German Workers' Party, the Nazis.

Germany did have one ally—Italy. Although Italy had a king, Prime Minister Benito Mussolini ruled the country as a dictator. In 1936 Italy and Germany signed a treaty of friendship. Mussolini described the treaty as a "Rome-Berlin axis." The alliance between Germany and Italy would later be known as the Axis powers.

TRYING TO AVOID WAR

In Britain and France, people were against more conflict. Political parties in these countries were divided on how to deal with the new threats to peace. When Hitler began flexing Germany's military muscle, Britain and France did their best to negotiate to try to prevent war. Negotiation often meant giving in to German demands.

In 1938 Germany was threatening Czechoslovakia. British Prime Minister Neville Chamberlain met with Hitler in Munich in an attempt to solve the Czech crisis. But that didn't happen. Germany, which had already invaded Austria, took over Czechoslovakia in 1939. Britain began to prepare for war.

Japan had been showing aggression against China since the early 1930s. In 1937 the Second Sino-Japanese War broke out between Japan and China, which led to Japan's takeover of large parts of China. U.S. leaders were worried about Japanese expansion, and tensions increased between the two countries.

THE EARLY DAYS

*B*ritain and France stood firm when Adolf Hitler and his armies invaded Poland on September 1, 1939. Two days later Britain and France declared war on Germany. The following spring Germany invaded Denmark and Norway. In May Germany unleashed its forces on the Netherlands, Luxembourg, Belgium, and France. Germany's rapid attacks were called the blitzkrieg, meaning "lightning war."

Britain immediately sent military aid to mainland Europe, but Paris fell to the Germans June 14, 1940. France was defeated, and the British forces were pushed back to the English Channel. A massive

fleet of British ships rescued many of the troops, but a German invasion of England was now a possibility. In London newly appointed Prime Minister Winston Churchill became the symbol of British resistance. In early June he told the British Parliament, "We shall fight on the beaches, we shall fight on the landing-grounds, we shall fight in the fields and in the streets, we shall fight in the hills, we shall never surrender."

BATTLES IN THE AIR

In order to invade England, the Germans needed to take control of the narrow English Channel and the air above it. German bombs rained down on British airfields and cities, especially London, in what was known as the Blitz. The bombing left many people dead, injured, or homeless.

During the summer Royal Air Force pilots fought the German air force, the Luftwaffe, over the skies of southern England in the Battle of Britain. More than 500 RAF pilots were killed, and the country was very close to defeat. Churchill praised the bravery of the British pilots, stating that "never in the field of human conflict was so much owed by so many to so few."

Instead of giving up, the RAF increased efforts against the Luftwaffe. The RAF scored a decisive victory September 15, destroying 55 German aircraft. Hitler canceled the invasion two days later, but the bombing continued until spring 1941. Throughout Britain 60,000 people were killed and 87,000 seriously injured during the Blitz.

Firemen worked to control fires during the Blitz attacks on London.

THE ROLE OF THE U.S.

Although not yet directly involved in the war, the United States sent ships, supplies, and weapons to Britain, angering Germany. German torpedoes hit the USS *Reuben James* October 31, 1941, making it the first American ship lost to enemy attack during the war.

In the meantime, the United States was keeping an eye on events in the Pacific and East Asia. Relations between the U.S. and Japan continued to worsen because of Japan's ongoing war with China. Both the U.S. and Europe were concerned about Japanese intentions toward Asian colonies—the American-ruled Philippines, French Indochina, the Dutch East Indies, and the British colonies of Hong Kong, Singapore, Burma, and Malaya. In September 1940 Japan signed a treaty with Germany and Italy, becoming part of the Axis powers.

CH. 3
1941:
THE ALLIES EXPAND

As Britain struggled to survive, Germany made its biggest

move yet. In June 1941 the German army launched Operation

Barbarossa, a massive invasion of the Soviet Union. Britain and the

United States offered help to the Soviet Union, leading the country

to join the Allies. Soviet leader Joseph Stalin was determined to

resist Germany, saying in July 1941, "The Red Army and Red Navy

and all citizens of the Soviet Union must defend every inch of Soviet

soil, fight to the last drop of blood for our towns and villages . . ."

German soldiers were successful during the early days of Operation Barbarossa.

The Germans didn't let Stalin's words stop them. They
advanced quickly, pushing the Soviet armies back and taking
huge numbers of prisoners. German soldiers moved toward
Moscow and Leningrad, Russia's major cities. The soldiers were
only 15 miles (24 kilometers) from Moscow at the end of 1941.
Leningrad would endure a siege lasting 872 days, in which it
is believed 1 million people died. Leningrad resident Nikolai
Markevich wrote in his diary January 24, 1942, "The city is dead
… Almost the only form of transport is sleds … carrying corpses
in plain coffins, covered with rags or half clothed … Daily six to
eight thousand die … The city is dying as it has lived for the last

half year—clenching its teeth." In Moscow a counteroffensive by the Soviet army eventually pushed the Germans back, relieving pressure on the capital city.

SURPRISE ATTACK IN THE PACIFIC

U.S. leaders continued to be concerned about Japan, but still tried to preserve peace. That changed the morning of December 7, 1941, when the Japanese attacked Pearl Harbor. The attack came in two separate waves and lasted about two hours. In addition to the 2,400 Americans killed, more than 1,100 were wounded. Four battleships and one training ship sank and four battleships were damaged. A bomb sank the USS *Arizona*, killing 1,177 of the 1,510 men aboard.

Ed Sheehan, an ironworker at the Pearl Harbor dockyard, witnessed the attacks. "When the second-wave planes came in," he wrote, "they appeared as if from out of nowhere, even soundless at first. They darted like angry birds at the *Nevada*, hitting her again and again. From a distance she seemed to shiver and shrug, but miraculously kept moving ... Then the destroyer *Shaw* was hit, out on the floating dry dock ...The ship appeared to disintegrate into a million pieces, becoming a gargantuan fireball. The blast sent scraps twisting and flying in all directions, for thousands of feet, in great slow-motion arcs trailing streamers of smoke. I was probably a quarter of a mile away, yet one of the pieces fell at my feet."

The attack was devastating, but there was one bright spot for the United States. The U.S. aircraft carriers, which would prove crucial

to the war effort, were out at sea that day. Although Pearl Harbor was a crushing blow, the U.S. Pacific fleet was still intact.

Japan later attacked Hong Kong, Singapore, Malaya, the Dutch East Indies, and the Philippines. The United States and Britain, along with several other countries, declared war on Japan. On December 11 Germany and Italy declared war on the United States. The war had become worldwide.

A Date That Will Live in Infamy

The day after the attack on Pearl Harbor, U.S. President Franklin D. Roosevelt spoke to a joint session of Congress. "Yesterday, December 7th, 1941—a date which will live in infamy—the United States of America was suddenly and deliberately attacked by naval and air forces of the Empire of Japan."

The attack was a great shock to the people of the United States and led directly to the country entering World War II. Many Americans had opposed getting involved in the war. After Pearl Harbor the American people were united in their determination to defeat the enemy and avenge the events of December 7.

President Franklin D. Roosevelt

THE TIDE TURNS

Once officially involved in the war, the United States quickly expanded its military. The U.S. sent more weapons and equipment to Britain, with the first U.S. troops arriving there in January 1942. The following summer U.S. air crews took part in air raids against the German military. American military vehicles and equipment also went to the Soviet Union to help in the fight against Germany.

The Soviets continued to bear the brunt of German aggression in Europe. The German army launched a new offensive, planning to capture the oil-producing areas in the Caucasus region. One roadblock to their plans was the city of Stalingrad, an important industrial and transportation center on the Volga River.

Soviet soldiers defended Stalingrad near the outskirts of the city.

STALINGRAD

The Battle of Stalingrad began August 23, 1942, and was one of
the bloodiest in history. As many as 2 million soldiers and civilians
were killed, wounded, or captured during the five-month battle.
German and Soviet soldiers sometimes fought hand-to-hand with
daggers and bayonets as they tried to gain control of city streets.
Soviet soldiers lived in bombed-out basements and set booby traps
for the Germans in abandoned buildings. The Germans captured
most of the city, but they often couldn't hold on to their gains. Areas
captured by German soldiers in daylight were usually retaken by
the Soviets during the night.

By December the German soldiers were surrounded. They
were cold and running short of supplies, even shooting and

eating their horses for food. On January 8, 1943, Soviet General Konstantin Rokossovsky demanded surrender in this message to the German army: "The situation of your troops is desperate. They are suffering from hunger, sickness, and cold. The cruel Russian winter has scarcely yet begun. Hard frosts, cold winds and blizzards still lie ahead. ... Your situation is hopeless, and any further resistance senseless."

The Germans rejected Rokossovsky's demand but couldn't hold out much longer. By February 2 all German leaders at Stalingrad had surrendered. More than 90,000 soldiers were taken prisoner, and many died as they marched in the subzero weather to Soviet prison camps. Only 5,000 would survive the war.

Stalingrad was the turning point in the war on the Eastern Front. The Germans would never have another significant victory in the East. Also, in summer 1943, the Soviets decisively beat the Germans at the Battle of Kursk.

THE ALLIES FIGHT BACK

The British and American air forces had begun their bombing campaign against Germany, but they were also determined to strike a blow in North Africa. In November 1942 the British scored a decisive victory over the Germans at El Alamein in Egypt. The battle was the Allies' first successful large-scale offensive against the Germans. Churchill wrote later, "It may almost be said, 'Before Alamein we never had a victory. After Alamein we never had a defeat.' "

An Allied soldier takes a German soldier prisoner at the Battle of El Alamein.

At the other end of North Africa, the Allies landed in Morocco and Algeria in early November 1942, attacking the Germans from two directions. The war in North Africa ended with the German and Italian surrender in May 1943, which allowed the Allies to threaten Italy from the south. In July 1943 the Allies invaded Sicily and then crossed into mainland Italy. The Italian government surrendered at the beginning of September. But the Allies still faced stiff resistance from German troops sent to Italy to stop the Allied advance.

FIGHTING IN THE PACIFIC

In Asia the Allies endured several Japanese attacks. The British colonies of Malaya and Singapore fell in early 1942, as did the American-held Philippines. The Dutch East Indies also fell to the

Japanese, and with the attack on Burma, even British-held India was vulnerable.

The Allies' situation in the Pacific began to improve in May 1942, when they forced Japan to retreat after the Battle of the Coral Sea. But it was the Battle of Midway in June that proved a real turning point. American forces destroyed about 300 Japanese aircraft and sank four aircraft carriers during the victory. Japan couldn't easily replace its lost aircraft and ships, which weakened its position in the war.

Allied forces also began a counterattack with a victory over the Japanese on the island of Guadalcanal in the Solomon Islands. Other Allied attacks throughout 1943 captured some Japanese-held islands, while bypassing others. The Americans called this strategy "island hopping."

Aircraft carrier USS Yorktown was badly damaged during the Battle of Midway.

THE WAR AT HOME

World War II resulted in the deaths of about 50 million people, including 30 million civilians. Another 35 million people were wounded and 3 million were missing. Bombing raids accounted for many civilian deaths. About 3 million people, most of them children, were evacuated from Britain's major cities to smaller towns and the countryside to keep them safe from bombing raids. A bombing victim from Liverpool recalled: "When morning came we left the shelter and made our way home. There was no home. All that was left was a pile of bricks. We had nowhere to live except the shelter, and that was to be our home for six months."

Children huddled outside the wreckage of their London home in September 1940.

LIFE UNDER OCCUPATION

Conditions for civilians in occupied countries were often harsh. Attempts to attack German soldiers or sabotage their authority were severely punished. But organized resistance groups sprang up in France, the Soviet Union, and other countries. French resistance groups attacked the German occupation forces whenever they could. They protected British pilots who had been shot down over France and helped them get back to Britain. They also gathered intelligence on the German army. In the Soviet Union fighters known as partisans operated behind German lines. They killed German soldiers, blew up trains and vehicles, and destroyed supplies that might be useful to the German occupiers.

BRITISH BLACKOUT

British cities were shrouded in darkness during the height of the German bombing campaign. Even the smallest flicker of light would serve as a signal to the bombers. Each night everyone had to cover their doors and windows with heavy blackout curtains, cardboard, or even paint. Street lighting was either turned off or dimmed and the light deflected downward. Vehicle headlights and traffic lights were also fitted with slotted covers to deflect light down to the ground.

Germany's political persecution of those they considered enemies, including Jews, had been well known before the war. But the full horror of the Nazi concentration camps was unknown or not believed by people in the West. Approximately 6 million Jews died during what was known as the Holocaust, along with several million people from other persecuted groups. They included political prisoners, Jehovah's Witnesses, disabled people, homosexuals, and people who were called gypsies.

In Asia huge numbers of civilians died during the ongoing war in China. Civilians also were killed during the first Japanese attacks and in the later Allied offensives. Life under Japanese occupation was often harsh. In both Europe and Asia, many civilians were killed or injured when Allied bombing raids targeted ports or factories used by Axis military in occupied countries.

1944-1945:

VICTORY

*I*n 1944 the Allied bombing campaign against Germany continued.

The Allies captured Rome, Italy, on June 4. But these events were

completely overshadowed by the massive invasion of Normandy,

France, June 6, 1944. Its official name was Operation Overlord, but

it is better known as D-Day.

D-Day marked the beginning of the end of the war in Western

Europe. Allied commanders had been planning a massive invasion of

France for two years. They knew they would be in for a tough fight.

Allied troops stormed a Normandy beach June 6, 1944.

A HUGE INVASION

The D-Day landings were a coordinated effort by Allied ground, sea, and air forces on five beaches in Normandy. The beaches were code-named Utah, Omaha, Gold, Juno, and Sword. Shortly after midnight June 6, Allied planes dropped paratroops deep behind enemy lines to attack the German army from the rear. The paratroops waited silently for daybreak, when the invasion from the sea would begin. At 6:30 a.m. the first Allied troops left their landing craft and waded 300 feet (91 meters) to Utah Beach.

It is estimated that more than 4,400 Allied troops died on D-Day, with thousands more wounded or missing. The heaviest casualties came at Omaha Beach, where German soldiers on bluffs above

the beach picked off many Allied troops before they could make it to shore. But Allied leaders had feared that casualties would be much higher. Despite the enormous loss of life, the invasion was considered a success.

Battles continued throughout the summer as the Allies advanced. Paris was liberated August 25, and in September Allied soldiers reached the borders of Germany, Belgium, and the Netherlands. The Allies also launched an invasion of southern France in August that forced the German army to retreat.

GERMANY TRIES TO REGROUP

Germany began a major offensive in Belgium and Luxembourg at the end of 1944. The Germans wanted to split the Allied forces and capture the port city of Antwerp, Belgium, through which supplies were reaching the Allied armies. Its official name was the Ardennes Offensive, but it is better known as the Battle of the Bulge. The German attack had created a bulge in the Allied front line.

The battle began December 16, 1944, and lasted more than a month. It was the largest land battle fought by the Americans in World War II, involving about 500,000 U.S. troops. At first the Germans were successful. Heavy snow and freezing temperatures prevented the Allied air forces from attacking German tanks. The Americans ran their trucks every half-hour to make sure they would start and even urinated on frozen weapons to thaw them. But by January the Americans had the upper hand, and the Germans were forced to retreat. About 80,000 American soldiers were killed,

Allied soldiers liberated Paris, France, in August 1944.

wounded, missing, or captured. Estimated German casualties were
between 60,000 and 100,000.

VICTORY IN EUROPE

After the Battle of the Bulge, the Allies entered Germany and
crossed the Rhine River the following spring. The German army's
position in the east wasn't any better. The Germans were in almost
continual retreat from Soviet attacks throughout 1944. In the fall
the Soviet army advanced into Romania, Hungary, Bulgaria, and
Poland. By April 1945 the Soviets surrounded the German capital
of Berlin. In the west the Allies marched relentlessly into the
heart of Germany. His country in ruins, Hitler committed suicide
April 30. The official surrender was signed in early May. The war
in Europe was over.

FIGHTING ON IN ASIA

In 1944 the United States had launched a major offensive in the
central Pacific, capturing the Gilbert, Marshall, and Mariana
islands, as well as Guam. The island of Saipan in the Marianas was
used as a base from which to launch air raids against the Japanese
mainland. The U.S. also invaded the Philippines, defeating
Japanese forces there the next year.

In February 1945 the Americans landed on the Japanese island of
Iwo Jima, which was captured with a tremendous loss of life. Almost
7,000 Americans died and more than 19,000 were wounded. An
estimated 23,000 Japanese soldiers were killed. U.S. Fleet Admiral
Chester W. Nimitz declared after the battle "among the men who
fought on Iwo Jima, uncommon valor was a common virtue."

U.S. Marines raised the American flag on Iwo Jima February 23, 1945.

U.S. troops landed April 1 on the island of Okinawa, only 340 miles (547 km) south of Japan. After nearly three months of bloody fighting, the Americans took control of the island June 21. About 110,000 Japanese soldiers were killed, along with 45,000 civilians. The Americans lost about 12,500 men.

DROPPING THE BOMB

The stubborn resistance of the Japanese was an important consideration when the Allies planned their next move. The U.S. B-29 bomber *Enola Gay* dropped an atomic bomb August 6 on the city of Hiroshima, immediately killing about 70,000 people. It was the first use of a nuclear weapon in warfare. The pilot, Colonel Paul Tibbets, remembered, "A bright light filled the plane. The first shock wave hit us. We were eleven and a half miles slant range from

NAVAJO CODE TALKERS

Spying was important to both sides during World War II. The Americans cracked the Japanese Imperial Navy's code early in the war, allowing them to read secret messages. The Japanese also broke some of the American codes. But one code was never broken—the Navajo American Indian language. The Navajo language was complicated, had no written alphabet, and at the time was understood by fewer than 30 non-Navajos. Differences in the tone of the speaker's voice or the way a word was pronounced could completely change the meaning. About 400 Navajo served the U.S. Marines as code talkers during Pacific battles.

A mushroom cloud formed after the bomb dropped on Nagasaki, Japan.

the atomic explosion, but the whole airplane cracked and crinkled from the blast. We turned back to look at Hiroshima. The city was hidden by that awful cloud ... mushrooming, terrible and incredibly tall."

Soviet forces invaded Japanese-held Manchuria in northern China August 8. The next day the U.S. dropped another atomic bomb on the city of Nagasaki, killing about 50,000. Harry Truman, who became U.S. president following Roosevelt's death in April, had been told of the tremendous destructive power of the atomic bomb. But he also knew that huge casualties were expected on both sides during an invasion of Japan. The decision to use the atomic

bombs was at least partly based on the desire to save American lives. The Japanese government agreed to end the war August 15.

Even before Truman's official announcement of the war's end, people were celebrating all over the United States. *Life* magazine commented that Americans seemed to feel "as if joy had been rationed and saved up for the three years, eight months, and seven days since Sunday, Dec. 7, 1941." In New York the largest crowd in the history of Times Square gathered to celebrate. Similar celebrations occurred in other Allied countries. The official Japanese surrender took place aboard the USS *Missouri* in Tokyo Bay September 2, Victory over Japan Day. World War II was over.

A famous photo of the Times Square celebrations appeared in Life *magazine.*

INDEX